"Most of us only aspire to make a profound difference in our time on this earth, but in 16 short years, Dana Pettaway fulfilled that goal. Before the accident that claimed her life, Dana lived a life of uncommon joy, pain and faith that continues to alter the lives of all who knew her or hear her story today. Dana's journal entries portray the thoughts, hope, and wisdom of a person who knew who she was and made choices to align her life with her deepest values. At the same time, she actively supported others whose backgrounds and beliefs were very different from her own, living out the love on which her faith was based.

This book offers a tangible model of God's amazing grace of transformation in one's life, and the difference a life filled with meaning can make. Dana's words will open your hearts."

Carol Munn
Dana's junior year English teacher

"This journal may come as a surprise to those who think of today's youth as selfish and materialistic. It will be an inspiration to those who yearn to instill spiritual values in the youth with whom they live or work.

After God's Own Heart will give you a glimpse into the spiritual life of a teenage girl who loved and sought after God with all her heart."

Kathleen Straker, M.Ed.
Co-author, *Study Without Stress* and *Vital Skills*

After God's Own Heart

The Spiritual Journal of
Dana Michelle Pettaway
A True God Chaser

Compiled by
Curtis and Janice Pettaway
With Foreword by Pastor Rod Parsley

After God's Own Heart
The Spiritual Journal of Dana Michelle Pettaway
A True God Chaser
Compiled by Curtis and Janice Pettaway
With Foreword by Pastor Rod Parsley

Printed in the United States of America

ISBN 9781613791875

Unless otherwise indicated, Bible quotations are taken from The Holy Bible, New Living Translation. Copyright © 1996, 2004, 2007 by Tyndale House Publishers, Inc.; The Holy Bible, New International Version® (NIV). Copyright © 1973, 1978, 1984 by International Bible Society Zondervan Publishing House; The King James Version of the Holy Bible (KJV); The Amplified® Bible. Copyright © 1954, 1958, 1962, 1964, 1965, 1987 by The Lockman Foundation. Used by permission. (www.Lockman.org); and The New King James Version, (NKJV). Copyright © 1979, 1980, 1982, 1984 by Thomas Nelson, Inc. Used by permission.

www.xulonpress.com

Foreward

Moses, in the only Psalm attributed to him, lamented the brevity of human life on earth. He compared our lives to a watch in the night, soon passed; to grass that flourishes for a season and then is withered; and to a tale that is told, the details of which become obscure with the passage of time.

But even in this extremity, we are not without hope, for God holds us securely in His hand, and we are never beyond the scope of His loving attention. We are weak, but His strength overcomes our weakness. Our lives are temporary, but the eternal God has provided a place for us that never changes and never passes away.

I am confident that the life story and testimony of Dana Michelle Pettaway will also endure. It will endure not just because of her radiant smile or her incandescent personality, and not only because of her determined devotion and radical commitment to a cause that she recognized was greater than life itself. I believe her testimony will continue to inspire those who hear it because she was thoroughly and completely connected to and captivated by the One who holds eternity in His hands—the same One who has made a place for her around His throne.

Even though her life ended far too soon, her legacy will continue. This record of her life will be a blessing and an inspiration to you.

Pastor Rod Parsley
World Harvest Church / Breakthrough
Columbus, Ohio

Dedication

To all who knew and loved Dana, and who played a role in her life. To all whose lives she touched in such a beautiful way. And to all who are enjoying the benefits of knowing her through hearing her story and reading this journal. May the memories never fade and your hope never wane, until we meet her again.

Contents

Prologue
Curtis Pettaway

About Dana Michelle Pettaway

Dana had always been an exceptional child. She could hold an adult conversation with me at age two, meaning that when I spoke to her, she not only listened but also synthesized what I said and came to the next logical conclusion. As she grew, Dana was scholastically impressive with a strong, competitive inner nature, but at the same time, a quiet humility wrapped up in a beautiful smile. As a child, she made it easy for Janice and me to be her parents, and we often joked that she was on autopilot.

However, fast forward into adolescence when we came face to face with the dilemmas that are so common to teenagers with respect to identity, sexuality, experimentation, and rejection of authority. It seemed as though she could look right through us, but we hadn't quite figured her out yet. No parenting manuals existed that could get us through this period.

We could only hold onto to the Lord for our strength and direction. In looking back, the single most-important thing we did was to expose Dana continually to the Lord and try to set godly examples. I remember someone telling me to "be firm, fair and consistent."

In our parental duo, Janice was what some would call the "good cop," while I often played the "bad cop" in our routine. To some extent, this was detrimental to my relationship with Dana during those years, because I was so busy enforcing that I didn't realize my little girl needed a loving dad to whom she could freely talk. I didn't realize that I was driving her away with my hardball attitude. Shortly after our family was moved to worship in a spirit-filled congregation with a dynamic youth ministry, Dana turned to the Lord, crying out to Him, and He answered her prayers. He would be her loving Father even when her earthly father fell down on the job.

My reconciliation with Dana came about two years prior to her death, after she had a life-changing experience at a Christian youth camp. Dana came home from camp filled with the Spirit of God and the desire to heal her relationship with me, her earthly father. For the first time, through the encouragement of the Holy Spirit, I realized the hell I had put Dana through, and I repented to God, as well as to Dana.

At age 15, Dana began to chase God with all she had. She was on fire, and in retrospect, Janice and I witnessed true God-seeking right in front of our eyes! She was in church on Sunday, at Monday night prayer, at Wednesday night Bible study, and in Friday night youth activities. She abandoned secular music in favor of contemporary Gospel and Christian artists. These were things that Janice and I weren't yet compelled to do.

We couldn't believe how she would seek her mother's opinion about the appropriateness of the clothes she wanted to buy or the modesty of the fit before she left the house. She was now a role model and wanted her appearance to reflect godly character. We were deliriously happy with her deliverance!

Before her junior year in high school, Dana decided to transfer to another area school. At the time, I wondered why she wanted to change schools. She was a straight-A student and a member of the sought-after girls' drill team. However, a few of Dana's friends, including her best friend, had also transferred the year before. Although Dana was popular, she felt somewhat isolated. Janice and I didn't realize what God had in store for Dana at her new school. We could tell she felt more comfortable in the new environment. She remarked that the rich mix of races and cultures was more of what "the world" was like, and she seemed to be embraced there. Dana was accepted onto the new school's drill team, but she gave it up soon thereafter to spend more time on praise dancing for the Lord.

Dana began to attend another high school's Student Venture Christian club meetings, which were held at our church on Monday evenings, and soon after, she and a friend from her new high school founded their own chapter of Student Venture. She mixed well with other students from various racial and ethnic backgrounds, and she loved talking about Jesus during club meetings. She could even witness in fluent Spanish! We could see that Dana's relationship with God was reaching new heights as she took on leadership roles both in church and at school. She truly had a passion for this God-given mission. A few days before her death in an auto accident at the age of 16, our pastor remarked that he could see God using Dana in a "mighty way," both now and in the future. We didn't realize at the time just how prophetic his statement was!

Dana and Dad

Introduction
Curtis and Janice Pettaway

To our family, church family, friends, those whose lives Dana touched, and those who are meeting her for the first time through the following pages, it is out of obedience to God's purpose that we share Dana's journal with you. We are confident that these writings were left to bear witness to what true devotion and love for Christ is: an example of the relationship He wants to have with each of us. Little did we know the depth of the call Dana had on her life. We were fortunate to discover her journal in her room a few short days after the accident. It is only in retrospect through her journal that we gain a glimpse into the inner workings of her heartfelt quest for God, her intimacy with Him and the realm of the influence given her to have an impact on others. The journal begins with her goals for the year 2000 and ends with an entry on January 16, 2001, two days before her death. It includes her personal reflections, prayers, scriptures, quotes from songs or poetry and original poetry.

Dana's final journal entry is a Psalm of reconciliation with God, written by King David. It is a Psalm of repentance, which opens the way for God's forgiveness and saving actions. David, referred to as "a man after God's own heart" (1 Samuel 13:13-14, Acts 13:22), recognized that the only good in him was the God in him. God uses those who are willing to step aside from their own need for ego building and self-gratification, to humble themselves before an Almighty God. In her April 27 journal entry, Dana herself stated that she was "a woman after God's own heart." Though her faith was shaken at times, she was fully surrendered to His will for her life and stood on the Word of God for her strength.

The writings of the journal have been typed for clarity and formatted, but not revised. However, some names have been changed to protect the privacy of others, and comments have been added to give more insight.

May you be blessed and encouraged by these writings, and spurred on to a life of greater service and a more intimate relationship with the Lord.

Habakkuk 2:2 (NIV)

**"Then the Lord replied: 'Write down the
revelation and make it
plain on tablets so that a herald may run
with it.'"**

The Journal
As Recorded By Dana Michelle Pettaway

Goals for 2000

1. Listen to God

> For what I should do next
> Who I should reach out to
> Where I need to be
> Major and minor decisions

2. Pray more often

> Wake up at 4:00 a.m. every morning to pray
> Fast once a week at least one meal
> Pray at night
> Try to stay in tune with God all day
> Remember to pray for others

3. Volunteer

Call hospitals
At church
Nursing homes

4. Maintain GPA

Study
Be determined

5. Have a boyfriend that does not interfere with my relationship with God

No sex
Better to have no boyfriend than to be torn from God
Listen to God

6. Have a Car

Take people to church
Take people places

7. Drink more water

8. Bring others to Christ

Car
Boldness

Things I Need to Improve On

1. Being Tactful
2. Praying for Others
3. Lying (being honest)
4. Listening to Others
5. Being Selfless
6. Being Bold in God
7. Having Faith

Prayers for the New Year

Perry	the Lord Bless and Guide his life
Aja	the Lord give her strength and make her an example to her family
Diana	the Lord show Himself strong and make His presence known in her life
Sonny	the Lord save him and show Himself strong in his life
Ashley	the Lord save her
Shawn	the Lord make Himself known and give him purpose
Rukiya	the Lord break down barriers in her life & repair her family
Temica	the Lord rescue her & save her & give her his peace & hope

April 2000

April 10, 2000

Take Back Everything God Gave To You

Variation: Take back what the devil stole

What this means to me: Take back hope, my child-hood, my family, friends, pureness, and smiles

Future Reference:

1. I want to deny my flesh and stop myself from future thefts of the devil.
2. God has purified me, and I want to devote my life fully to him.
3. I feel that I really have been called to the ministry by God.

Praises: Thank you Lord for

1. Opening up my eyes
2. Showing me love
3. Freeing me and giving me my calling

April 14, 2000

The Lord Is a God of a Second Chance

Variation: Despite all my wrongs, I have a second chance.

What this means to me: The Lord is a gracious, loving God, who gives His children the desires of their hearts. He let me into Cy-Falls* to have a fresh start.

Future Reference:

1. Take advantage of fresh start at Cy-Falls.
2. See why the Lord has me there – follow His calling – Be obedient

Praises: Thank you Lord for

1. Giving me a second chance
2. Blessing me and opening the door
3. Being merciful
4. Showing me your true love

*(Dana transferred from her high school to *Cypress Falls High School.)*

April 17, 2000

What Is Man That Thou Art Mindful of Him?

Variation: Could an awesome God find common ground within?

What this means to me: Just to know that He delights to be with me, fills my heart with joy. He could have me as his servant, yet He wants to call me His friend.

Future Reference:

1. Keep in mind that He is greater and it is a privilege to be His friend.
2. Always communicate with Him because that is what He desires.

Praises: Thank you Lord for

1. Being my friend, loving me
2. Blessing me with your Presence
3. Showing me my purpose

April 24, 2000

God Will Make a Way When There Seems to Be No Way

Variation: God will provide all you need

What this means to me: God will make a way for the things that He will have me to do in this life. He will open and close doors and provide what seems impossible, to guide my life.

Future Reference:

1. When God opens a door, don't worry about how He's going to do it, just go and watch Him provide.
2. Don't worry – pray – have faith

Praises: Thank you Lord for

1. Loving me
2. A job, a ride to and from
3. Providing not only a car, but a way to keep it
(Dana was thanking God for a job and a car He had not yet provided.)

April 27, 2000

Lord, I come to you right now praising your name and magnifying your name, because you are holy. So many things I don't understand, but you do, because you are God, Lord Almighty. I come humbly and boldly before your throne – already having faith – that you would speak to my heart and send your Holy Spirit, stronger than ever, to rule my life. I trust you, and I ask for your Perfect Will to ascend and guide me. You are my rock and my everything. Continue to break me, so that I can be built up in you. Break me of pride & vanity. Purify my soul. Help me to be a blessing to your people. *Lord, I am a woman after your own heart.* Seeking your wisdom and your guidance. I love you, and I praise your name. I am forever your servant; just show me what you would have me to do. Use me to comfort your hurting people. Send me to tell the message of Hope and Life.

May 2000

May 1, 2000

Believing in Things Not Seen

Variation: Speaking things that are not, as though they were

F – A – I – T - H

What this means to me: *Believe and trust in God. Don't limit him. He is the one who spoke the earth into existence. He is capable of all things if you only believe.*

Future Reference:

1. No longer will I walk in fear or be weak or allow my flesh to control me
2. I will stand BOLDLY and trust in the word of God
3. I will tell my mountain to move in Jesus' name

Praises: Thank you Lord for

1. Loving me
2. Faith, Wisdom and Strength

Fast

GOALS:

1. **Car by the end of May.** The Lord provided me with a job and a new school; I trust that He will provide my transportation as well.
   * Despite us being told August, I Believe and have Faith in God that it* will be here by the end of May.

(*Dana was speaking of a car that was to be gifted to her by a relative.)

2. **Perry: Spirit-filled in the Lord.** The Lord told me to hold on. Now I stand firm on that promise.
   * I will not allow the Devil to continue to steal from me.
   * Despite the circumstances and what everyone else thinks, I believe that God will use Perry for something big. I trust that the Lord will fill him with his Holy Spirit and bless his life. I also trust that the Lord will guide Perry through His perfect will.

(Perry was Dana's boyfriend. He was not committed to God, but Dana looked beyond the surface and saw his potential in the Lord. Many times, in her reference of Perry, she spoke in faith – claiming that his character and relationship with God was

strong and devoted. She was committed to praying for him and seeing the best in him in every circumstance.)

3. **Patrice and her mother**

- Vanity is something that needs to be broken down. The devil uses so much to block us from our blessings.
- Satan steals. He does not want to see us victorious. Her mother was healed from drugs. Satan brought the addiction back to control her mind.
- I believe that God will set her mother free from addiction and break Patrice from vanity so that God can use her. God uses everyone that is willing.
- I pray that He will fill their hearts and comfort them and bless them with strength and love.

4. **God's Will for My Life**

- Lord you've brought me through so much, you've blessed me beyond my wildest dreams
- You've loved me, held me, taught me, corrected me, and given me wisdom.
- I pray that you will bless me with humbleness, strength and wisdom.
- I pray you will strengthen your Holy Spirit over me until it reigns over my flesh.
- Give me boldness so that I can teach & mentor & talk about you.

May 5, 2000

Lord, I know that you can do all things. You are the God that spoke the world into existence and parted the Red Sea. You are the same God who used Saul –(Paul) to preach your Word. Thank you for your love. Through Jesus Christ, I have this power. Thank you for your love. What is man that thou art mindful of him? You are my everything. Come into my life so that I may be able to do your will. Lead me & guide me daily. I love you. Amen

May 8, 2000

Vision: The Lord has guided me toward business. I believe that I will open a center for pregnant women.

Mission: My mission is to help God's hurting people. Help to lead the misguided and hurting to God.

Gift: God has recently given me the gift of compassion. My flesh is naturally selfish and self-absorbed. Compassion has overtaken me.

Plea: Lord, I want you to guide and bless me. This is huge, and I can't do it on my own. Fill and continually guide me.

Praises: Lord I Praise you for

1. Your love and guidance

2. Lord, I thank you for Perry. You have truly blessed me with a pure-hearted individual. You have given me a strong desire and love for him. I thank you for your guidance. Please forgive me for questioning you and losing faith. I know that you will bless us as we continue to do your will. I love you.

3. I thank you for showing me my mission in life, to help the hurting. Help me to learn how to dedicate my life to those I don't know. Continue to give me compassion. I need it from you to fulfill what you have called me to do. I love you, I praise you.

June 2000

June 1, 2000

The Lord is truly teaching me patience. I am happily enduring all things. Not right now when I want it, but right on time when God wants it. He's my best friend.

Jesus Is the Savior

He has come to set us free from the evil and sin that bind our minds and life.

Lord and Savior. He rescues us from the chains that bind the way that we think.

"And I, the Son of Man have come to seek and save those like him who are lost." Luke 19:10

"Look, I am sending you out as sheep among wolves. Be as wary as snakes and harmless as doves."
Matthew 10:16

June 11, 2000

Jesus Is Lord

Dear Lord,

You will reign eternally as you do now. I will bless your Holy name. Thank you for holding and keeping me all of this time, I love you most of all because you loved me when I did not even love myself. Please forgive me for the horrible things that my flesh does. Cleanse me and help me to realize when I am doing the slightest thing motivated by an unclean heart. Purify me, Oh Lord, make me like you. You are my everything, and I will forever sing your praises. Holy, Sweet Jesus. Allow your Holy Spirit to flow through me. I love you Lord. Change me. Make and mold me. Help me to exhibit your love and kindness. I need you every day. I thank you for what you have shown me through Perry. I love you and I trust you to do your will. I see that you are molding him as well. Despite the circumstance, I look at you. You are teaching me patience. Still, I continue to wait with joy—depending on you for my next ride. I love you. Thanks. Not once have I not had a ride anywhere that I needed to go. My heavenly Father, provider, Prince of Peace, fall on me. You are awesome. You will reign forever.

June 17, 2000

Lord,

Today, my heart is broken. Today, I'm truly being broken down. My other half is missing. I love him so much more than a boyfriend or a son. Oh Lord, please take control of the situation; Jesus please intervene. Today, a young couple that [went] to Cy-Falls were killed. I'm so frightened for Perry. I feel so afraid and scared. Lord, please give me your peace. I don't want to worry; I want to rest with the assurance that he is home sleeping. I have no control, so I trust it all to you. Oh Lord, help him not to go down the same path as his dad. Lord, you told me to hold on. Where are you? Where are you now that I am crushed and in a hopeless situation? I can only trust that you are still at work and telling me not to worry. I can only trust that you are guiding Perry in your gentle hands. I love you, Lord, and I praise your holy name. Even now, I must fight my flesh to praise you. I must remember that you are the same God that parted the Red Sea and the same God who spoke this world into existence. Lord, thank you for comforting me. You told me that Perry was the one, so I know that you would not let anything happen to him. You are an awesome God. I praise your name now and forever.

All for Good

Romans 8:28
"And we know that God causes everything to work together for the good of those who love God and are called according to His purpose for them."

I trust in you, Lord
Now and Forever

Presence of God

Hebrews 10:22 (NLT)
"Let us go right into the presence of God, with true hearts fully trusting him…

God Keeps Promise

Hebrews 10:23 (NLT)
"Without wavering, let us hold tightly to the hope we say we have, for God can be trusted to keep His promises"

Hebrews 13:5
"Stay away from the love of money; be satisfied with what you have, for God has said, "I will never fail you. I will never forsake you"

Thank you, Lord, for sending your Holy Spirit to me. I love you and I praise your Holy name. I love you so much. I trust that you are in control and that you hold my future. Thank you for taking away all of the worry and the hurt. I know that you are working on both Perry and me at the same time. Greater is He that's inside me. Praise your Holy name. Greater is He that's in me.

June 19, 2000

Deliberate Sin

Hebrews 10:26
"Dear friends, if we deliberately continue sinning after we have received a full knowledge of the truth, there is no longer any sacrifice that will cover these sins."

Endurance-Promises

Hebrews 10:36
"Patient endurance is what you need now, so you will continue to do God's will. Then you will receive all that he has promised."

Faith

Hebrews 11:1
"What is faith? It is the confident assurance that what we hope for is going to happen. It is the evidence of things we cannot yet see."

Obey

Hebrews 13:17
"Obey your spiritual leaders, and do what they say. Their work is to watch over your souls, and they are accountable to God. Give them reason to do this with joy and not with sorrow. That would certainly not be for your benefit."

Discipline

Hebrews 12:5-6
'"...My child, don't ignore it when the Lord disciplines you and don't be discouraged when he

corrects you. For the Lord disciplines those he loves, and punishes those he accepts as his children.'"

Refresh-Stand

Hebrews 12:12-13
12 "So take a new grip with your tired hands and stand firm on your shaky legs.
13 Mark out a straight path for your feet. Then those who follow you, though they are weak and lame, will not stumble and fall but will become strong."

Lord,

I trust you. I love you. You are my peace, my hope, and my joy. I love you so much, My Savior. You loved me when I did not love myself. You saved me from myself and loved me. What an awesome God. Thank you, Lord, for the second chance at life. I will forever serve you. Forever. My heavenly Father, my Redeemer. Praise and glory be to God. Lord, I trust you, and I will stay true to your will and to your way. My prayer is that you will mold me into something that you can use. Make me, mold me. I love you. Hold me while Perry is gone. Help me to remain faithful and strong in you. I know that you have me here for a reason. I trust you with my life. Take me into your arms as your child. Hold me and comfort me. I love you. My heavenly Father, Lord over my life. My everything. My flesh tries to make me afraid. But I will not allow it. I love you, My God.

You're So Good! So Generous! So Kind! Thank you, Jesus, my high priest.

Today, Perry is going to rehab (2 months). I trust that this is your will.

"All things happen for the good of those who love God and are called according to His purpose for them." Romans 8:28

June 20, 2000

Bad Actions-Deny God

Titus 1:16
"Such people claim they know God, but they deny him by the way they live. They are detestable and disobedient, worthless for doing anything good."

Role of Women

Titus 2:4-5
"These older women must train the younger women to love their husbands and their children, to live wisely and be pure, to work in their homes to do good, and to be submissive to their husbands. Then they will not bring shame on the word of God."

No Fear

2 Timothy 1:7
"For God has not given us a spirit of fear and timidity, but of power, love and self-discipline."

June 21, 2000

Trust God

2 Timothy 1:12
"...For I know the one in whom I trust, and I am sure that he is able to guard what I have entrusted to him until the day of his return.

Right Living

2 Timothy 2:22
*"Run from anything that stimulates youthful lust. [Follow anything that makes you want to do right.] Pursue faith and love an*d peace and] *enjoy the companionship of those who call on the Lord with pure hearts."*

Preach

2 Timothy 4:2
"Preach the word of God. Be prepared, whether the time is favorable or not. Patiently correct, rebuke and encourage your people with good teaching."

Lord   6/21/00

Thankyou for your many blessings.
Looking to you instead of the
circumstance helps out a lot. I
know that you are going to
bless me and that you have
already got an answer to every
one of my prayers. I trust that
you have already fixed it. I
love you because you are a God
who works everything out for
the good of those who love
you and are called according
to your purpose for them.
I know that you love me
and that I am your child
thankyou in advance for
the victory.

Strengthening When We're Weak

"So take a new grip with your tired hands and stand firm on your shaky legs. Mark out a straight path for your feet. Then those who follow you, though they ARE WEAK and lame, will not stumble and fall but will become stronger."(Hebrews 12:12-13)

Variation: Don't give up! Stand firm on His promises and hold tightly to the hope we say we have. *

*(*Based on Hebrews 10:23)*

What this means to me: I go through what, to me, is a lot of stress and grief. God tells me to stand firm and cling to him. Not to give up even though my hands are tired and my legs are shaky. "Hold on" – the famous words that God spoke to me – Hold on to the Hope I say I have.

Future Reference:

I will no longer allow my "tiredness" to be an excuse of my letting go. I will go after God and his promises fiercely. Through the storm – I will cling & stand firm.

Praises: I thank you Lord for

1. Your Word
2. Speaking to my heart
3. Your love, kindness and mercy

4. All that you are
5. Your power and patience

Hebrews 12:12
"So take a new grip with your tired hands and stand firm on your shaky legs. Mark out a straight path for your feet. Then those who follow you, though they are weak and lame, will not stumble and fall, but will become strong!"

1. Daily struggles and life will beat us down, we will get tired and may become weary (rains on just and unjust). We get emotionally and spiritually beat down as well.

   Hope - Hold

   2. "Take a new grip with your tired hands…"

   Hebrews 10:23
   "Without wavering, let us <u>holdtightly</u> to the hope we say we have, for God can be trusted to keep his promises." Hebrews 10:23

New Grip on Hope. God is Hope. He is Love.

3. And Stand Firm on your shaky legs

   God's Armor
   Stand Firm

   Ephesians 6:11
   "Put on all of God's armor so that you will be able to stand firm against all strategies [and tricks] of the devil."

49

Resist Enemy Stand Firm

Ephesians 6:13
"Use every piece of God's armor to resist the enemy in the time of evil, so thatafter the battle you will be standing firm."

* Must put on all of God's armor

The Last Days

2 Timothy 3:1-5, 4:3-4
In the last days, there will be very difficult times:
- people will love only themselves and their money
- they will be boastful and proud
- they will be disobedient to their parents and ungrateful
- they will consider nothing sacred
- they will be unloving & unforgiving
- they will slander others & have no self-control
- they will have no interest in what is good
- they will betray their friends, be reckless, be puffed up w/pride and love pleasure
- they will no longer listen to right teaching
- they will want teachers who tell them what they want to hear

June 23, 2000

1 Thessalonians 5:16-18
"Always be joyful. Keep on praying. No matter what happens, always be thankful, for this is God's will for you who belong to Christ Jesus."

Winning Others/ Wives

1 Peter 3:1-2
"In the same way, you wives must accept the authority of your husbands; even those who refuse to accept the Good News. Your godly lives will speak to them better than any words. They will be won over by watching your pure, godly behavior."

Beauty/ Wives

1 Peter 3:4
"You should be known for the beauty that comes from within, the unfading beauty of a gentle and quiet spirit, which is so precious to God."

The Spirit

Ephesians 1:14
"The Spirit is God's guarantee that he will give us everything he promised and that he has purchased us to be his own people. This is just one more reason for us to praise our glorious Lord."

Proverbs 4:26 and Hebrews 12:13
"Mark out a straight path for your feet…"

Isaiah 26:7
"But for those who are righteous, the path is not steep and rough. You are a God of justice, and you smooth out the road ahead of them."

Proverbs 4:25-27 (AMP)
"Let your eyes look right on, and let your gaze be straight before you. Consider well the path of your feet, and let all your ways be established and ordered aright. Turn not aside to the right hand or to the left; remove your feet from evil."

Hebrews 12:12-13
"Then those who follow you, though they are weak and lame, will not stumble and fall, but will remain strong."

Philippians 1:14
"And because of my imprisonment, [many Christians] here have gained confidence and became bolder in telling others about Christ."

June 24, 2000

New Attitude

Ephesians 4:22-24
"Throw off your old evil nature and your former way of [life, which is corrupted by] lust and deception. Instead, there must be a spiritual renewal of your thoughts and attitudes. You must display a new nature because you are a new person, created in God's likeness – righteous, holy and true."

Anger

Ephesians 4:26-27
"And 'don't sin by letting anger gain control over you'. Don't let the sun go down while you are still angry, for anger gives a mighty foothold to the Devil."

Do Good

Ephesians 5:16
"Make the most of every opportunity for doing good in these evil days."

Don't Trust Humans

Isaiah 2:22
"Stop putting your trust in mere humans. They are as frail as breath. How can they be of help to anyone?"

Be Humble

Isaiah 2:15
He will break down every high tower and wall.

Wounded - Healed

Isaiah 53:5
"But he was wounded and crushed for our sins. He was beaten that we might have peace. He was whipped, and we were healed!"

No Weapon

Isaiah 54:17
"But in that coming day, no weapon turned against you will succeed…."

God's Thoughts

Isaiah 55:8-9
"'My thoughts are completely different from yours,' says the Lord. 'And my ways are far beyond anything you could imagine. For just as the heavens are higher than the earth, so are my ways higher than your ways and my thoughts are higher than your thoughts."

God Sends Word

Isaiah 55:11
"It is the same with my word. I send it out, and it always produces fruit. It will accomplish all I want it to and it will prosper everywhere I send it."

Live Like Christ

1 John 2:6
"Those who say they live in God should live their lives as Christ did."

June 26, 2000

This world offers

1 John 2:16-17
"For the world offers only the lust for physical pleasure, the lust for everything we see, and pride in our possessions. These are not from the Father. They are from this evil world; and this world is fading away, along with everything it craves. But if you do the will of God, you will live forever."

God Listens

1 John 5:14
"And we can be confident that he will listen to us whenever we ask him for anything in line with his will."

Your Heart

1 John 5:21
"Dear children, keep away from anything that might take God's place in your heart."

June 27, 2000

Last Times

Jude 1:18
"That in the last times there would be scoffers whose purpose in life is to enjoy themselves in every evil way imaginable."

Natural Instincts

Jude 1:19
"...They live by natural instincts because they do not have God's Spirit living within them."

Jude 1:22-23
"Show mercy to those whose faith is wavering. Rescue others by snatching them from the flames of judgment..."

Rescue

1 Peter 1:9
"Your reward for trusting him will be the salvation of your souls."

Lord,

Thank you for your mercy and abounding love. Thank you for your kindness and generosity. Thank you for inviting me, a dirty sinner, into your family. I love you and your gentle corrections and teachings. Thank you for guiding my footsteps and holding my hand. Thank you for the sword of truth that is the only weapon we have to fight against the Devil. Thank you for being my friend. I love you Lord. You are mighty and powerful. All authority belongs to you. Nothing else matters but your love and your grace. You have kept me through everything. Continue to anoint my life and bless my actions. Lord, please continue to hear my prayers. Lord, send your Holy Spirit to forever fill me and filter me, convicting me of all wrongs and evil in my body. Jesus, thank you for suffering for me. Thank you for having me in mind when you hung from the tree. You were cursed so that I could be blessed. I love you and I long to serve you. Show me where you would have me to go. Please direct my path, O Lord. Show me where you want me to be. I am a willing servant. Prepare me for my calling and equip me with all I need. I love you because you are faithful! I love you because you are God.

Proverbs 17:3
"Fire tests the purity of gold and silver, but the Lord tests the heart."

Trials - Test faith

1 Peter 1:7
"These trials are only to test your faith, to show that it is strong and pure. It is being tested as fire tests and purifies gold – and your faith is far more precious to God than mere gold. So if your faith remains strong after being tried by fiery trials, it will bring you much praise and glory and honor on the day when Jesus Christ is revealed to the whole world."

Backsliding

1 Peter 1:14-15
"Obey God because you are his children. Don't slip back into your old ways of doing evil; you didn't know any better then. But now you must be holy in everything you do, just as God – who chose you to be his children – is holy."

Judge

1 Peter 1:17
"...He will judge or reward you according to what you do….."

Evil - Soul

1 Peter 2:11-12
"Dear brothers, you are foreigners and aliens here. So I warn you to keep away from evil desires because they fight against your very souls. Be careful how you live among your unbelieving neighbors…."

June 29, 2000

Lord,

I pray that you would really anoint this camp, and I pray that you would speak to my heart. Lord, I love you with everything in me! Fill my heart and completely take me over. You are my all. Please take control of my life and guide my path. Open my heart and continue to break me down so that I can be built up in you. I love you and I trust you.

June 30, 2000

Discovery Camp
(Discovery Camp is a Summer Youth Bible Camp held at Burchfield Ministries in Columbus, Texas. Dana went with her church youth group.)

Isaiah 53, Matthew 5, Romans 10

Psalm 37:5
"Commit everything you do to the Lord. Trust him, and he will help you."

Isaiah 53 (Prophesies Jesus and His crucifixion)
- 780 yrs. before it happened
- 32 details – 100% fulfilled
- Law of compound probability – one chance in 68,719,476,736

Things Jesus Paid for:

1. Your acceptance with God and man
2. Your grief
3. Your sorrow
4. Your sin and guilt
5. Your peace
6. Your healing

Dana at Discovery Camp

Fast

Lord, I put my faith completely in you. I love you and I praise you. I dedicate myself unto you. You are my rock and my strong tower. I pray that in these three days I would grow in my faith for you, learn to dedicate myself to you and be purified through you.

1. Have children

Hebrews 11:11 (AMP)
"Because of faith also Sarah herself received physical power to conceive a child, even when she was long past the age for it, because she considered God, who had given her the promise, to be RELIABLE and TRUSTWORTHY and TRUE to his word."

Hebrews 11:6 (AMP)
"But without faith it is impossible to please and be satisfactory to Him. For whoever would come near to God– most believe that God exists and that He is the rewarder of those who earnestly and diligently seek Him (out)."

Psalm 130:5-6 (AMP)
"I wait for the Lord, I expectantly wait, and in His word do I hope. I am looking and waiting for the Lord more than watchmen for the morning, I say, more than watchmen do for the morning."

Proverbs 31:30 (AMP)
"...but a woman who reverently and worshipfully fears the Lord, she shall be praised."

Proverbs 9:10 (AMP)
"The reverent and worshipful fear of the Lord is the beginning of Wisdom, and the knowledge of the Holy One is insight and understanding."

Psalm 128:1 (AMP)
"Blessed is everyone who fears, reveres and worships the Lord, who walks in His ways and live according to His commandments."

Matthew 6:33-34 (AMP)
"But seek (aim at, strive after) first of all His kingdom and His righteousness (His way of doing and being right), and then all these things taken together will be given you besides.
So do not worry or be anxious about tomorrow, for tomorrow will have worries and anxieties of its own. Sufficient for each day is its own trouble."

Lord, I thank you for your precious word that you have laid upon my heart. Lord, you promised that if I turned from my sinful nature and lifted my eyes unto you, that you would answer my prayers and that I would delight in you. I praise your holy name. O, God my father, you promised that if I do these things that the ones in whom I intercede for, would be saved! You are such a mighty God. I will continue to sing your praises every day of my life. I will hide your word in my heart and carry out your will. I open myself up as a vessel.

- ★ "….Lay up His words in your heart." (Job 22:22 NRSV)
- ★ Return to Him
- ★ Lay gold in dust
- ★ Make Lord your gold
- ★ Delight in Him
- ★ Lift up your face
- ★ He will hear your prayer
- ★ Decide & decree a thing, it will be established
- ★ He will give light
- ★ Lifts up humble

Job 22:30 (AMP)
"He will even deliver the one who is not innocent, yes, he will be delivered through the cleanness of your hands."

July 2000

July 1, 2000

The Little Girl

I feel so sorry for that little girl. She was so hurt and so lost. If only she had known that there was a Jesus, the little girl that cried and hurt so bad. Be patient little girl, the living God has something special just for you because he loves you so much. Yes, even you were born for greatness. Yes, you are so precious. The same God that created the universe loves you. He's your dad who wants to hug you and love on you. You can call him daddy and sit on his lap. He's your daddy and he wants to spoil you and read to you at night. He's at all of your games and still takes time to hold you when you're hurting.

Little girl, smile. For there is hope. You are special to God. He sees you and loves you so, so much. Even though you're independent, your dad will still be there to catch you when you fall. He says that you're worthy of his love, he says you're worthy of his grace, yes, even you. Don't cry and don't lose hope. Your daddy loves you very much.

Lord, I thank you for loving and keeping that little girl. Thank you for bringing her up and showing her your love. Thank you for healing all of the hurt and loneliness in her heart. Thank you for being her daddy, daddy.

Dana at age 14

July 2, 2000

The Head

Deuteronomy 28:13
"If you listen to these commands of the Lord your God and carefully obey them, the Lord will make you the head and not the tail, and you will always have the upper hand."

If my people...

2 Chronicles 7:14
"Then if my people who are called by my name will humble themselves and pray and seek my face and turn from their wicked ways, I will hear from heaven and will forgive their sins and heal their land."

Power of Christ

2 Corinthians 12:9
"...So now I am glad to boast about my weaknesses, so that the power of Christ may work through me."

July 3, 2000

Lifestyle

Matthew 3:8
"Prove by the way you live that you have really turned from your sins and turned to God."

Unjust/ Just

Matthew 5:45
"...For he gives his sunlight to both the evil and the good, and he sends rain on the just and on the unjust, too."

Treasure

Matthew 6:21
"Wherever your treasure is, there your heart and thoughts will also be."

Eye

Matthew 6:22-23
"Your eye is a lamp for your body. A pure eye lets sunshine into your soul. But an evil eye shuts out the light and plunges you into darkness. If the light you think you have is really darkness, how deep that darkness will be!"

July 4, 2000

Two Masters

Matthew 6:24

"No one can serve two masters. For you will hate one and love the other, or be devoted to one and despise the other. You can't serve both God and money."

Primary Concern God's Kingdom

Matthew 6:33

"And he will give you all you need from day to day if you live for him and make the Kingdom of God your primary concern.:

Log in Eye

Matthew 7:5

"Hypocrite! First get rid of the log from your own eye; then perhaps you will see well enough to deal with the speck in your friend's eye."

Gateway to Life

Matthew 7:14

"But the gateway to life is small, and the road is narrow, and only a few ever find it."

Persistence

Matthew 7:7

"Keep on asking and you will be given what you ask for. Keep on looking, and you will find. Keep on knocking and the door will be opened."

All Revealed

Matthew 10:26-27
"For the time is coming when everything will be revealed; all that is secret will be made public. What I tell you now in the darkness, shout abroad when daybreak comes..."

Stay Alert

Matthew 26:41
"Keep alert and pray. Otherwise, temptation will overpower you. For though the spirit is willing enough, the body is weak."

God's Gifts

Matthew 7:11
"...if you sinful people know how to give good gifts to your children, how much more will your heavenly Father give good gifts to those who ask him."

Luke 12:32
"So don't be afraid, little flock. For it gives your Father great happiness to give you the Kingdom."

Fruit of Labor

Ecclesiastes 3:13
"And people should eat and drink and enjoy the fruits of their labor, for these are gifts from God."

God's Plan

Jeremiah 29; 11-12
"For I know the plans I have for you" says the Lord. "They are plans for good and not for disaster, to give you a future and a hope. In those days when you pray, I will listen."

Matthew 10:37-39*

Those who love their father or mother more than they love me are not wanting to be my followers. Those who love their sons or daughters more than they love me are not wanting to be my followers. Whoever is not willing to carry the cross and follow me is not worthy of me. Those who try to hold on to their lives will give up true life. Those who give up their lives for me will hold on to true life.
*(paraphrased)

Desires

Psalm 37:4
"Take delight in the Lord, and he will give you your heart's desires."

Bad Conduct

Philippians 3:19
"Their future is eternal destruction. Their god is their appetite, they brag about shameful things, and all they think about is life here on earth."

Philippians 3:12
"...But I keep working toward that day when I will finally be all that Christ Jesus saved me for and wants me to be."

July 5, 2000

Lord,

I just don't understand it. Why is everyone else's time right now? Their time to laugh and be carefree with their boyfriend, their best friend, and their car. I don't understand it! Did I do something wrong? Why can't my boyfriend be on his way to pick me up? Why is there always so much pain and struggle? I know that this is your perfect will. Maybe tomorrow is the day in your will for me where I will smile – then again maybe not. I'm trying to trust you and be patient. I'm trying to keep the faith and rely on your word. My soul hurts, Lord. Thank you for being the Lord of my life. I love you with all of my heart. Praises be to God forever and ever. Amen.

Faith/Power

Philippians 3:9-10
"And become one with him. I no longer count on my own goodness or my ability to obey God's law, but I trust Christ to save me. For God's way of making us right with himself depends on faith. As a result, I can really know Christ and experience the MIGHTY POWER THAT RAISED HIM FROM THE DEAD." (emphasis added.)

Philippians 3:21
"He will take these weak mortal bodies of ours and change them into glorious bodies like his own, using the same mighty power that he will use to conquer everything, everywhere."

Philippians 2:10-11
So *"that at the name of Jesus every knee will bow, in heaven and on earth and under earth, and every tongue will confess that Jesus Christ is Lord, to him be glory of God the Father."*

Colossians 1:11
"We also pray that you will be strengthened with his glorious power so that you will have all the patience and endurance you need...."

Name of Lord

Luke 10:17
"When the seventy-two disciples returned, they joyfully reported to him, 'Lord, even the demons obey us when we use your name.'"

1 John 4:14
"Furthermore, we have seen with our own eyes and now testify that the Father sent his Son to be the Savior of the world."

July 9, 2000

Job 22:23
"If you return to the almighty and clean up your life, you will be restored."

July 13, 2000

Spirit of God

1 John 4:4
"...The Spirit who lives in you is greater than the spirit who lives in the world.'

Romans 8:15
"So you should not be like cowering, fearful slaves. You should behave instead like God's very own children, adopted into his family – calling him "Father, dear Father.""

Romans 8:26
"And the Holy Spirit helps us in our distress. For we don't even know what we should pray for, nor how we should pray. But the Holy Spirit prays for us with groanings that can't be expressed with words."

Lord,

I love you with all of my heart. Today, I found out that the thing I long for the most is threatened. Lord, this one is from me. I pray that when it is "time" and I am married that I will be more than able to have children. You are my dad who owns all things. I know that you are bigger than the "bad" news I received today. But, Lord, if I can't have kids, I will serve you anyways. I trust that this is your will for me. You know the desires of my heart – the curly-headed girl, the boys, the family. Lord, I will trust you. You said that those who delight in you – that they would receive their hearts desires. But, if not, you have already blessed me with so much. I praise your name because you are the God of my life. I will serve you. I will, no matter what. Hell or high water, you are my God.

I am every bit whole. Greater is He who is within me than he who is in the world. For God causes everything to happen for the good of those who love Him and are called according to His purpose for them. For God has not given us a spirit of fear but one of Love, Power and Self-discipline. I will have children for God delights in giving us the desires of our hearts.

(On the morning of this entry, a doctor told Dana that she had a medical condition that might prevent her from having children).

Romans 6:16
"Don't you realize that whatever you choose to obey becomes your master? You can choose sin, which leads to death, or you can choose to obey God and receive his approval."

Romans 5:3
"We can rejoice, too, when we run into problems and trials, for we know that they are good for us – they help us learn to endure."

Love Endures *1 Corinthians 13:7*
"Love never gives up, never loses faith, is always hopeful and endures through every circumstance."

Help me to be this way with Perry. How can I say I love him and not show it? I must first change the way I approach and really love him before I can expect anything from him.

July 16, 2000

Lord,

Thank you for life and thank you for your love. You are more than enough to cover my sins and more than enough to patch my heart. You are more than enough joy, peace, and love to last me a lifetime. Thank you, Lord. You truly are all that I need. Your mercy, your grace, your kindness. Thank you for the revelation of love and what it means. Thank you for your unconditional love. If you showed it to us, why shouldn't we show it to others? Thanks for your love. You truly are a God of all things. You really know everything. Thank you, Lord. Thank you, Lord. Help me to love more like you. Help me to remember true love. Please help me to love.

1 Corinthians 13:4-7
"Love is patient and kind. Love is not jealous or boastful or proud or rude. Love does not demand its own way. Love is not irritable, and it keeps no record of when it has been wronged. It is never glad about injustice but rejoices when the truth went out. Love never gives up, never loses faith, is always hopeful and endures through every circumstance."

July 17, 2000

Lord,

Thank you for being the Lord over my life. I love you with all of my heart. You are the God of a second chance, Jehovah Jireh, Jehovah Nissi, and Jehovah Shalom (my prince of peace). You are sooooo awesome. Today you once again showed me how real you are!!! You are alive and real right now. What a privilege, for you to dwell inside of me. I love you, O magnificent God. How Great Thou Art. Lord, I pray that I would be on fire for you until the day that I die. I pray that I would trust, love and hunger for you until I stop breathing. You are my God and I will ever praise you. There is so much wisdom and joy in being your servant. It is awesome to be a child of God. Walking in the light. No longer do I have to feel my way around in the darkness because I have the light of God burning in me. Let my hunger never run out. Help me to love others. Help me to genuinely love others, for I know that it's important. Lead me to my husband. I trust you with all of my heart. Speak to me about Perry, let me know Lord. I seek to stay in your will.

1 Corinthians 10:13

Escape

"...And God is faithful. He will keep the temptation from becoming so strong that you can't stand up to it. When you are tempted, he will show you a way out so that you will not give in."

God Makes Seed Grow

1 Corinthians 3:7
"The ones who do the planting and watering aren't important, but God is important because he is the one who makes the seeds grow."

No Compromise

Psalm 119:2-3
"Happy are those who obey his decrees and search for him with all of their hearts. They do not compromise with evil, and they walk only in his paths."

Few Words

Proverbs 17:27-28
"A truly wise person uses few words; a person with understanding is even-tempered. Even fools are thought to be wise when they keep silent, when they keep their mouths shut, they seem intelligent."

Name of Lord

Proverbs 18:10
"The name of the Lord is a strong fortress; the godly run to him and are safe."

Gentle Answer

Proverbs 15:1
"A gentle answer turns away wrath, but harsh words stir up anger."

Tongue

Proverbs 18:21
"Those who love to talk will experience the consequences, for the tongue can kill or nourish life."

July 29, 2000

I pray that you could help me with this pain. I don't understand and it hurts. I want my grandmother, or at least to see a picture. Lord, I need you; I need you to hold me. All those years, you carried me. All of those years you watched over me constantly. You saw the hurt and you had already planned to take it away. What a privilege to be able to trade my sorrow and my pain. Thank you, Holy Spirit, for being the Counselor. I have learned to lean on you, Lord. You taught me young and you taught me well. Thank you for the work that you are doing in Perry. I know that you are going to continue to do exceedingly and abundantly above all I could ask or think. He will not turn out like his dad, but On Fire for you. What a blessing to have a guy who fully trusts in you. What a blessing to have a companion who shares a similar hunger and love for God. I thank you. I love you and I trust you. Forgive me of my sins and please wipe me clean.

In Jesus Name, Amen

(Dana's grandmother had passed a few days earlier, and Perry was in Juvenile Detention. Although this was a seemingly low point in her life, Dana remained steadfast and continued to speak with prophetic faith about Perry.)

July 30, 2000

The Important Things

Lord, thank you for showing me what matters most:

A love for God
A hunger and reverence for God
Love!!!
Patience
Kindness
Faithfulness
Joy
Family
Friends
Happiness
Trust
Faith
Power
Self-control
Wisdom

August 2000

August 1, 2000

How Perfect is God?

How perfect is God?
He knows exactly what we need
When we need it
How we need it

How perfect is God?
He carves a pathway for our feet
We just have to fall in the grooves
He always carries us through

How perfect is God?
To save us through no works of our own
To make a place in heaven as our home

How perfect is God?
Always on time
Always providing
Always listening
Always forgiving

August 2, 2000

Lord,

I trust you, I really do. I need you. Please don't allow sadness to fill my heart. I feel so alone. I completely lean on and need you. I do trust you to work in mine & Perry's life. You're the only way that it will work. I walk by faith knowing that everything is going to work for the good of those who love you. I won't allow Satan to get me down and try to make me walk by sight. For I know the one in whom I trust and I am sure He's able to guard all I have entrusted to Him. Please help me to cope and make it through this school year. I love you so much. You're all that I have and need in this world. I love you daddy. I know that you only want what's best for me.

꙳ Always,
Dana

Jesus, you're the one who makes me whole
Jesus, you're the comfort of my soul
Jesus, you heal our broken hearts forever
I run to you, hold me in your arms forever

August 3, 2000

Lord,

I thank you, gracious, heavenly Father, for all of your promises. I will seek you first. I will follow after you with all of my heart. I love you. Why should I fear when I have Jesus by my side? The Maker of heaven and earth. I thank you, Heavenly Father, for allowing Perry to leave early. It looks like there's no way, but thank you, Jesus, because I have a daddy who can do all things. My dad orchestrates every facet of life. He can surely let Perry out early. I love you Jesus. I praise your Holy Name.

ᴢ✎ Always,
Dana

Lord,

I feel so lonely. I don't even know what to do; so lonely and let down. I don't understand why I'm the one without any friends and without a boyfriend. I trust that you have someone for me. But who? Where is my other half? Where am I? What am I doing here? Why isn't there happiness? Lord, I need you, I really need you. You promised that you would never leave me and I know that you won't leave anyone forever. I need you so much now. Who will ever want me? Who will ever love me? Who will ever think that I am special? When will you send "my" guy? Who will hold me and stand with me? When will I ever stop crying? When will I stop feeling so empty? It really hurts. I wish your joy would overcome me. I wish that my faith would be increased, Lord. I trust you and I know that all things are working together for my good. Lord, I surrender and I give it up, all of it. I am a giant failure. I completely and totally need you. Please forgive me for my sins. They don't fill my emptiness, only you can.

September 2000

September 16, 2000

Lord,

I will give up Perry if it is not in your will. I will release him. More than anything, I want you and your will for my life. I trust you to make a life for me, Lord, if it is not meant to be, please take away my desire for Perry and separate us. I give him completely up, I trust that you will guard him and make a wonderful life for him. But, I want you more than I want him, so, if it's not in your will, please separate us.

I will never forget this awful time, as I grieve over my loss. Yet, I still dare to hope when I remember this:

Lamentations 3:20-24
"The unfailing love of the Lord never ends! By his mercies we have been kept from complete destruction. Great is his faithfulness; his mercies begin

afresh each day. I say to myself, 'The Lord is my inheritance; therefore, I will hope in Him!'"

Lamentations 3:25-27
"The Lord is wonderfully good to those who wait for him and seek him. So it is good to wait quietly for salvation from the Lord. And it is good for the young to submit to the yoke of his discipline."

Lamentations 3:31-32
"For the Lord does not abandon anyone forever. Though he brings grief, he also shows compassion according to the greatness of his unfailing love."

Lamentations 3:55-57
"But I called on your name, Lord, from deep within the well, and you heard me! You listened to my pleading; you heard my weeping; yes, you came at my despairing cry and told me, 'Do not fear!'"

Lord,
    This is really tough. I trust in you. But I don't know what to do. I know that you are telling me that Perry is the one. He thinks that he needs time away from me to grow in you. It hurts, but you are helping me to let go. I know that you have not taken him away forever, that you have plans for the two of us. I will look to you, the Maker of Heaven and Earth.

Please end my loneliness. Help me to grow in you. I know the woman that you want me to be; I can see her. Right now, you are strengthening me and preparing me. Thank you for helping me to control my anger and sadness. I seek your face and the freedom that comes from truly knowing you. I love you.

October 2000

October 7, 2000

Lord,

I bless your name for you are the Creator of Heaven and Earth. The lover of my soul, Father, I need you now. I never want to stop hungering for you and I never want to stop praying to you. Help me to be consistent through the good and the bad times. Right now, my soul and heart are broken and I hurt. I pray that you would fill me with you and your presence. Lord, I magnify your name and I thank you for being my Father. Just as surely as you parted the Red Sea, you will bring me through.

* God has to be first

Heed the Word

James 1:25 (AMP)
"But faultless law, the law of liberty, and is faithful to it and perseveres in looking into it, being not a heedless listener who forgets but an active doer (who obeys), <u>he shall be blessed in his doing</u>."

October 21, 2000

Lord,

I thank you for giving me a heart and a desire to work with women. Lord, I pray that you would help this desire to gain in the direction of your will. I pray that you would nourish this desire and provide the necessary open doors. Show me you. I seek you. I love you. I need you. Lord, I praise your name. You would want to bless even me, after everything that I've done and all that I've said. I'm still in amazement that you care about even me. If you can use anything, you can use me. I need you; I'm hungry for you. I want you and I love you. You truly are everything that I need. Thank you for my life. Thank you for my life.

ॐ Always,
Dana

Today I make the decision to
be humble
To lower my pride, release
my selfish ambitions
Lord, your will
Be it to clean floors and
be single all my life
I am no one. I am
a servant to you.
What a privilege to
live, to breathe, to pray

Your presence is wonderful
and full
I seek you, but in an humble
and quiet way
In the respectful, yet fearful
way, I need you
Sovereign and awesome
God
You are the Holy One
I bow my head in Respect

October 28, 2000

Wallowing In Me

I reach out and reach in
I cry out and cry within
I yearn and I feel
Lord I seek you
I need you

The unimaginable
The expanse of your omnipotence
Accept me, you know it all
As I fight and battle
Against my own self

Give me your strength
You see me wallowing in me
You see me lost inside of me

I yearn and I feel
I cry out and cry within
I reach out and reach in
for you

Help me to devote myself to you. Teach me to
pray and teach me to trust in you. I want to give
myself to you; I want to give myself to you. Save me.
I need your salvation. Your grace. I need you. But
most of all, you know what I need. I'm not worthy
to even hear your voice. But I trust that you will see

me. I trust that you will guide me. Lord, you know me. I love you.

Seeking God First

Psalm 130 (AMP)
"Out of the depths have I cried to You, O Lord. Lord, hear my voice; let Your ears be attentive to the voice of my supplications. If You, Lord, should keep account of and treat [us according to our] sins, O Lord, who could stand? But there is forgiveness with You [just what man needs], that You may be reverently feared and worshiped. I wait for the Lord, I expectantly wait, and in His word do I hope. I am looking and waiting for the Lord more than watchmen for the morning, I say, more than watchmen for the morning. O Israel, hope in the Lord! For with the Lord there is mercy and loving-kindness, and with Him is plenteous redemption. And He will redeem Israel from all their iniquities."

Psalm 130:1
"Out of the depths have I cried to you, O Lord."

- Out of the depths – from the inner being – deep within from what He is made of (soul)
- In the midst of his "trouble," of his "darkness," of His "depths" hecries out!
- not after he came through, but OUT OF the depths

When Jeremiah used these words
- Depths – mire, dungeon (Lamentations 3:55)
- took Jeremiah & cast him into the dungeon or cistern pit – no water – only mire (Jeremiah 38:6)

* OUT OF DEPTH – (not from w/out) cried OUT of

Psalm 130:2
"Lord, Hear my voice; let your ears be attentive to the voice of my supplication"

- <u>Supplication</u> – humble and honest entreaty; humble prayer to a deity for mercy and, or <u>special blessing</u>
- Not want, whim, or desire, but HUMBLE request – begging
- Establishes God as deity – more than equal – when you supplicate to him

Psalm 130:3
"If you, Lord, should keep account of and treat [us according to our] sins; O Lord, who could stand?"

Establishes the fact that

- His "depth" may be the cause of his actions
- He is not DESERVING of help – that he is nothing (humbling self)
- [The] Lord is in control of our destiny and our life – He controls outcome

Psalm 130:4
"But there is forgiveness with you [just what man needs], that **you may be reverently feared and worshipped."

Matthew 6:33
"But seek first of all His kingdom and His righteousness, and then all these things taken together will be given you besides." (NIV)

1. How can we seek God first?

- Aim at and strive after Him
- His way of doing & being right

Deuteronomy 10:12 (AMP)
"And now, Israel, what does the Lord your God require of you but reverently to fear the Lord your God ..."
That is "to walk in all His ways and to love him..."

2. What are His requirements and right ways?

- to walk in all his ways and to
- love Him, and to
- serve the Lord your God with all your [mind and] heart and with your entire being

We are now His "Israel" – his chosen people.

- The #1 requirement is to reverently fear the Lord.
- Reverent – awe, dread, fear

- Helps us to recognize how holy He is
- MUST be done in one's heart – evidences

  A. Walk in His ways
- Ten Commandments
- Hebrews 12:12-13

  B. Love Him
- showing fear

  C. Serve Him With
- all mind
- all heart
- and with entire being
- entire being –
  - ★ what are your hands doing?
  - ★ what is your body doing?

  D. Deuteronomy 10:16
- "So circumcise the foreskin of your [minds and] hearts & be no longer stubborn and hardened."

Psalm 130:5
"I wait for the Lord, I expectantly wait, and in His word do I hope."

[Isaiah 40:31]
"Those that wait upon the Lord He shall renew their strength."

Lamentations 3:26
".. it is good that we should hope in and wait quietly for the salvation of the Lord."

Lamentations 3:27
["And it is good for people to submit at an early age to the yoke of his discipline."]

Lamentations 3:28 (AMP)
"Let him sit <u>alone</u>, <u>uncomplaining</u> and <u>keeping silent</u> [in hope], because [God] has laid [the yoke] upon him (<u>for his benefit</u>)."

Romans 8:28
("And we know that God causes everything to work together[a] for the good of those who love God and are called according to his purpose for them")

Lord,

I love you. Thank you for your freedom and true life. You have blessed me beyond my wildest dreams. I pray that through your forgiveness, that I might become a true worshipper of you. Allow me to truly seek your face. Help me to die to my flesh and earthly desires enough to seek your holy face. You are awesome. Today I'm realizing that I need your salvation everyday and that it is a continual process. Thank you Jesus, you truly are the Saviour! Today I am sad, but from out of the depths, Lord, I cry to you. I wait patiently and quietly for your strength.

Ruth 3:11 (AMP)
"And now, my daughter, fear not. I will do for you all you require, for all my people in the city know that you are a woman of strength. (worth, bravery, capability)."

Psalm 143:8
"Let me hear of your unfailing love to me in the morning, for I am trusting you. Show me where to walk, for I have come to you in prayer."

Lord please show me what you would have me to do, guide my feet with your word. I trust you with all of my heart, you are my God and your love is unfailing.

Jeremiah 15:16(AMP)
"Your words were found and I ate them; and your words were to me a joy and the rejoicing of my heart, for I am called by your name, O Lord, God of hosts."

Psalm 51:6 (AMP
"Behold, you desire truth in the inner being; make me therefore to know wisdom in my inmost heart.")

Moving Forward

Hebrews 11:15-16

If they [those mentioned in Hebrews 11:15-16] had been thinking with remembrance of that country from which they were emigrants, they would have found constant opportunity to return to it. But the truth is that they were yearning for and aspiring to a better and more desirable country, that is, a heavenly [one]. For this reason, God is not ashamed to be called their God, for He has prepared a city for them.

November 2000

November 25, 2000

Hebrews 11:15 (AMP)
"If they had been thinking with remembrance of that country from which they were emigrants..."

- We are emigrants from the world
- We should not have our minds on the things of the world (Romans 12:2)
- Don't look backwards when God has moved you forward
- Don't try to drag any remembrance of where you came from with you
- If God delivered you from it, your mind should not be thinking with remembrance to it
- [homesick remembrance]

They would have found countless opportunities to return to it

- The opportunities are there, they are open
- Only if you are in homesick remembrance are they visible

- One must renew their mind in order not to be homesick
- Once one is homesick, it can easily end up in "return"
- How one's life continues to go in circles after God delivers them
- You <u>must</u> move forward; you <u>must</u> renew your mind

Otherwise, it will be a cycle. But the truth is that they were yearning for and aspiring to a better and more desirable country, that is a heavenly [one]

- The "better and more desirable place, thing is heavenly, meaning heaven ordained.
- The "aspiring" and "yearning" were due to faith, true faith in the word of God.
- These aspirations and this mindset kept them from missing the past and wanting to digress.

For this reason, God is not ashamed to be called their God, for He has prepared a city for them.

- The ultimate place to get to is heaven; as God moves us from place to place, don't look back, look up.
- God loves for us to have faith – although He is God – He's not ashamed of us when we have faith.
- For the reason that they aspired for His heavenly place He was not ashamed of them.
- Aspire towards the place simply because He prepared it.

Proverbs 4:23 (AMP)
"Keep and guard your heart with all vigilance and above all that you guard, for out of it flow the springs of life."

Proverbs 4:25-27(AMP)
"Let your eyes look right on [with fixed purpose] and let your gaze be straight before you. Consider well the path of your feet and let all your ways be established and ordered aright. Turn not aside to the right hand or to the left, remove you foot from evil."

Choices

Proverbs 4:25 (AMP)
"Let your eyes look right on… and let your gaze be straight before you…"

Keyword: Let

- God has given you freedom of choice, but you must allow this to be your desire.
- It is possible – but it is a choice – something that one wills to do

Eyes

- The eyes guide you – you will go in the direction that they call you
- Learn to guard what you watch
- Eyes represent your focus and desires in life

- Eyes must be fixed on something
- Changing fixation
- Fixed on everything
- Physical direction

Gaze

- True intent or focus
- Ideal place of location (goal)

Colossians 3:1-3 (AMP)
"If then you have been raised with Christ, aim at and seek the [rich, eternal treasures] that are above, where Christ is seated at the right hand of God and set your minds on what is above [the higher things], not on the things that are on earth. For [as far as this world is concerned] you have died and your new, real life is hidden with Christ in God."

Mindset, Dead to World

Psalm 37:3(AMP)
"Trust in the Lord and do good, so shall you dwell in the land and feed surely on His faithfulness, and truly you shall be fed."

Psalm 37:4 (AMP)
"Delight yourself also in the Lord, and He will give you the desires and secret petitions of your heart."

Psalm 37:7(AMP)
"Be still and rest in the Lord; wait for Him and patiently lean yourself upon Him, fret not yourself because of him who prospers in his way, because of the man who brings wicked devices to pass.'

Psalm 37:24 (AMP)
"Though he falls, he shall not be utterly cast down, for the Lord grasps his hand in support and upholds him."

Psalm 37:5(AMP)
"Commit your way to the Lord…trust …also in Him and He will bring it to pass."

December 2000

December 18, 2000

(This is a prayer list of things and people for which Dana committed prayer. The "club" she refers to is a chapter of Student Venture, a Christian club that Dana co-founded and led at her high school.)

- Unsaved members of club
- Lost in the school
- Strength of the Leaders
- Strong, well-planned lessons
- Always be for glorification of God
- Victor remains strong
- Pastor Steve continues to rely on God
- Holy Spirit would invade our church
- We would focus on seeking God
- Give me a hunger for God
- Let me have a desire to do His will
- Brandi, Kandis, Ashley, Rafael, LeKendra, Patrice, Andi, Perry, Valerie, Lance

- Reassure me about calling and future
- Cleanse me; get rid of all that's not of God

A sign Dana made for Student Venture

As a Matter of Life and Death

Colossians 3:1-8 *(AMP)*

3:1 *"If then you have been raised with Christ... aim at and seek the [...treasures] that are above..."*

- raised above situations above circumstances, above sin, and above the group of the devil
- raised to heavenly places – from your death
- Aim at – What's your aim in life? – What are you looking for? A husband, a job, a car?

3:2 What is at center of target? *"And set your minds and keep them set on what is above... not on the things on the earth."*

- Romans 12:2
- Psalm 37:4-7
- Proverbs 4:25-27
- Hebrews 11:15

3:3 *"For as far [as this world is concerned], you have died, and your [new real] life is hidden with Christ in God."*

- You have ceased to exist in this world's affairs
- You have no connections to worldly things – not bound by their standards

"When Christ, who is our life, appears, then you also will appear with Him in [the splendor of] His glory." — 3:4

- Christ is our life because we were resurrected <u>with</u> Him – there is no other way to life. Without His resurrection, we are still bound to this world and dead
- If you're a born again Christian you better recognize that Christ IS YOUR LIFE – or else you're still in the grave
- For the present time we are hidden in God w/ Christ

Be humble, meek and mild, it's not our time to shine – Christ was hidden

- The Glorious day is when he appears, then we will shine

"But now put away and rid yourselves [completely] of all these things: anger, rage, bad feelings towards others, curses and slander, and foulmouthed abuse and shameful utterances from your lips." — 3:8

- No longer a child of this world – but new life in Jesus
- Must recognize that Jesus is your life.

Luke 1:20 (AMP)
"...But my words are of a kind, which will be ful-filled, in the appointed and proper time."

Luke 1:37 (AMP)
"For with God nothing is ever impossible and no word from God shall be without power or impossible of fulfillment."

Luke 5:5(AMP)
"And Simon (Peter) answered, Master, we toiled all night (exhaustingly) and caught nothing (in our nets) but on the ground of your word, I will lower the nets (again)."

Luke 5:6 (AMP)
"And when they had done this; they caught a great number of fish and as their nets were [at the point of] breaking."

December 23, 2000

Dear Lord,

I have toiled all night, exhaustingly, with Perry and my relationship. For 3 long years have I tried and I was convinced that it could not work. But on account that your words are of a kind, which will be fulfilled, in the proper time, I will lower the nets again. For I know that with God nothing is ever impossible and no word from God shall be without power or impossible of fulfillment. For you told me to hold on and that you were going to do this, but your way. Let it be done to me according to what you have said.

Lord, you said in your word in Jeremiah 33:3 that if I prayed to you, that you would answer me and show me things that I did not know. Show me my calling and please confirm about Perry and I. I give my life to you and I seek to know your will. Break me down and make me like you want me. Teach me to pray and fast and seek your throne. I'm waiting for my answer from you. It may be that you have called me to evangelize and it may be that Perry will be my husband.

ॐ Always,
Dana

December 24, 2000

Level/Smooth

Luke 3:5 (AMP)
"Every valley and ravine shall be filled up, and every mountain and hill shall be leveled; and the crooked places shall be made straight, and the rough roads shall be made smooth."

Lord, I pray that you would level my pride, fill my voids with faith and healing, make my sinful ways holy, and smooth out the rough spots of my personality. Change me; I give my heart completely to you.

Last Praise Dance, Christmas 2000

1 Thessalonians 5:18 (AMP)
"Thank [God] in everything [no matter what the cir-
cumstances may be, be thankful and give thanks], for
this is the will of God for you [who are] in Christ
Jesus [the Revealer and Mediator of that will]."

Lord, I vow to trust you. You are the most important thing in life – I would give it all up for you, my
savior.

Luke 1:36 (AMP)
"And listen! Your relative Elizabeth in her old age
has also conceived a son, and this is now the sixth
month with her <u>who was called barren</u>")*
(*Dana underlined this passage for emphasis.)

December 26, 2000

Luke 1:38(AMP)
"Then Mary said, Behold, I am the handmaiden of the Lord, let it be done to me according to what you have said and the angel left her."

Luke 1:45(AMP)
"And blessed... is she who believed that there would be a fulfillment of the things that were spoken to her from the Lord."

Lord, I trust you and I stand on your word. You will come through. Perry is saved and preaching your word. He is spirit-filled and blessed. I will hold on and I will trust you, my Lord, my God. I bless your name. I pray that you would speak to me while in Atlanta. Change me, refresh and renew me. I expect there to be a mighty move of God.

(Dana was on her way to an "Impact 2000" Conference in Atlanta, which trains students to reach their friends for Christ).

December 27, 2000

Finishing Well
(Notes made on the talk given by Bryan Crawford)

1 Corinthians 9:24-27
Addressing the Stoppers

Finishing Well is the challenge committed to:

1. Excellence – Verse 24
Run: speaks of mature (attitude) – give your all
Misnomer about salvation – is FREE but not CHEAP

2. Endurance – Verse 25
Competes: agonize – presupposes pain and problems
* If you want to get big, you must pick up something heavy

3. Integrity – Verse 26
Preached: announce the rules – cannot live contrary to teachings – no prize – bridging gap between/ what we say & how we live

Lord,

I come broken before you. I leave everything else aside. I seek your face. I seek your glory. I desire you and you alone. Help me to maximize my brokenness so that I can see you. I present myself as a sacrifice. I love you and I need you. You are my God in whom

I will trust. I give myself and my life to you. Work your will in my life. Help me to put idle things aside in order to do your will. Lord, I praise and worship you as King and as the One that is in control. I love you and I delight in you. Let your love shine out through me. Not that I may get the glory, but that you may. You are my father in Heaven, and in you alone will I trust. Some men trust in doctors, others in money, but I will put my trust in the Lord.

Everything that I have experienced, I place it in your hands. You are my God and you have guided me through my life. You've held my hand and carried me. I know you, your love, and your Grace. Not one time have you failed me. Yes, I will trust in you. Yes, I will fear you. Yes, I will worship you. Yes, I will delight in you.

Make me pleasing to you.

Who Are You Fighting For?

How much of life is really based on Christ? John 11

Grace and Mercy flow from Heaven
Your Words oh God fill my mind
And your love encompasses me
How I long to worship
How my soul follows hard after thee
You alone are the King of Glory
And your faithfulness do I see

Fasting

Joel 2:12 (AMP)

Joel 2:12

"Therefore also now, says the Lord, turn and keep on coming to Me with all your heart, with fasting, with weeping and with mourning [until every hindrance is removed and the broken fellowship restored."]

Good 'n Plenty

1. Faithful Warriors - 1 Timothy 1:11
   There will always be struggle between flesh and spirit. Must fight a good fight.
   a. placed persons – stay in your lane
   b. point persons – "only one"
   c. prophetic persons – tell it like it is
   d. pure persons – lifestyle

2. Faithful Worshippers - Romans 1:25
   a. no sex
   b. no status
   c. no stash

3. Faithful Workers - 2 Thessalonians 1:3-12
   a. home
   b. hard
   c. hell

4. Faithful Walkers - Romans 10:14-21
   a. tell everybody

   ★ God has called us to be faithful

War-Time Realities

No suffering no crown

1. Crowned in the midst of suffering
   - Thorns (Genesis 3:17-19) – crowned with
   - Curse on Adam – Christ bore curse
   - Bled when crown placed

2. Jesus is not manipulated by the crowds (his servants)
   - Cannot manipulate God
   - God is king and sovereign authority

3. Sometimes looks like we're defeated in presence of enemies
4. People will party in the presence of Jesus
   - If [he] cared for others while in humiliation, [he] will care for us in supreme moments

2 Corinthians 2:14-17
Have a determination and a will

Must choose Jesus over sin each and every day

Romas 8 last paragraph

Must bring:

1. The <u>attitude</u> of triumph
   Christ always leads us in <u>His</u> triumph
   a. The war has already been won
   b. The victory is in 3-dimensions – past, present, future – triumph is daily
   ★ What God starts, he takes care of and finishes.
   c. It's time to celebrate

2. The <u>aroma</u> of triumph
   Different odors
   a. Scent – draws you
   b. Smell – flee

3. The <u>authority</u> of triumph
   Pillars of authority
   a. Integrity – Transparency
      Peddler – bootleg wine dealer (not watered down)
      Moral honesty
      If you're cheap wine, say you're cheap wine
   b. Sincerity
   c. Authenticity
      Force and power of the original

The most amazing thing about you is that you saved me from myself. When I was wandering around in the pitch-blackness of night, you saved my soul. I could not tell up from down, and the path that I should take appeared to be hidden. Oh, how you rescued me from both hells. Any God that could transform me must be real. Any God that could have reached down to me must be the One and Only Savior.

January 2001

January 1, 2001

But I Do Now

S he was groping, stumbling her way through the dark. She was lost and turned the wrong direction. This girl, this girl. She had no way out because she was darkness and death. She cried so long and so hard because she was the problem, and it consumed her. Her Father watched and thought, "How long will you deny my light and my love and my cross?" However, she could not hear and would not hear. Darkness, deception, lust, and corruption were her; they consumed her. She felt for so long in the dark. Searching for love and approval. Searching for protection and security. Searching for her dad. She bled loud and long. Her open wounds were more pain than she could bear. No earthly comfort was to be found. So she stumbled and fell, bled and cried deep inside. Pain flowed from her mouth and pervaded her heart. She was beaten down to the ground, down to her knees, down to submission. But it's not okay to hate "God"; it's not okay to worship pain, and it's not all right to dance in sin. Had she not been drowning so deep she would have seen so much. Had she not been wallowing in the murky waters of hunger she could have been satisfied. Little did she know that there was a God that loved her. Little did she know that she had a Father that wanted to hold her in His lap, kiss her on her cheek, and show His love. She had no clue that there was a hope and a light in His cross. But I do now. I praise you Father for rescuing me. Be ye exalted for coming down, Jesus, to save my soul. You are the King of Kings and the lover of my soul. You took away all of my pain. You took on my hurt and gave me love. And you satisfied my hunger.

January 8, 2001

Heavenly Father

You do not have to be overwhelmed.
You do not have to be weighed down
By the demands of others.
You only have to love God and enjoy
The freedom of being His child.
Tell me about deadlines, yours,
And I will tell you mine.
Meanwhile our Father looks down.
Meanwhile the air is fresh; there is a new day,
The bees hum, the roses bud, and the sun gleams.
Meanwhile your soul longs
For that which you were truly created.
Whoever you are, no matter how overwhelmed,
The Lord offers Himself to your longing soul,
He calls to you as a father to a child,
Loving and clear –
Over and over announcing your true place
In His Kingdom.

—Dana Pettaway

Andi,   1/10/00

    Hey sweetheart! My soul is grieved because it appears as though we have lost one. I challenge you to encourage and love her more than ever. Help her to once again experience the love of Christ. If we can save one girl from having sex, and getting pregnant all of this would be worth it. I we could educate one young man on how to stand up and be an uncompromising man of God - it would all be worth it. I sacrifice myself and all that I am to God in order that I may be used to save one. My soul is grieved. My soul is grieved. We must never cease to encourage, support, uplift, and rebuke. The Lord has sent this as a wake up call to STAND up, put on His armour, and fight. We may have problems, but we must remain strong because they are NOTHING compared to the hell that is breaking out all around us. Andi, we can not sit down, can not get discouraged, can not yet overwhelmed. My soul is so grieved. It hurts so bad. These are my girls. And this is what the devil wants to do to them. These are His daughters. And this is what the devil wants to do to them. These are our friends. And this is what the devil wants to do to them. I WILL NOT STAND BACK. *Love,*
Dana

Written to one of the leaders in her
Student Venture club.

January 16, 2001

Psalm 51 (AMP)
1. Have mercy upon me, O God, according to your steadfast love; according to the multitude of your tender mercy and loving-kindness blot out my transgressions.

2. Wash me thoroughly [and repeatedly] from my iniquity and guilt and cleanse me and make me wholly pure from my sin!

3. For I am conscious of my transgressions and I acknowledge them; my sin is ever before me.

4. Against you, you only, have I sinned and done that which is evil in your sight, so that you are justified in your sentence and faultless in your judgment.

5. Behold, I was brought forth in [a state of] iniquity; my mother was sinful who conceived me [and I too am sinful].

6. Behold, you desire truth in the inner being; make me therefore to know wisdom in my inmost heart.

7. Purify me with hyssop, and I shall be clean [ceremonially]; wash me, and I shall [in reality] be whiter than snow.

8. Make me to hear joy and gladness and be satisfied; let the bones which you have broken rejoice.

9. Hide your face from my sins and blot out all my guilt and iniquities.

10. Create in me a clean heart, O God, and renew a right, persevering, and steadfast spirit within me.

11. Cast me not away from your presence and take not your Holy Spirit from me.

12. Restore to me the joy of your salvation and uphold me with a willing spirit.

13. Then will I teach transgressors your ways, and sinners shall be converted and return to you.

14. Deliver me from bloodguiltiness and death, O God, the God of my salvation, and my tongue shall sing aloud of your righteousness (your rightness and your justice).

15. O Lord, open my lips, and my mouth shall show forth your praise.

16. For you delight not in sacrifice, or else would I give it; you find no pleasure in burnt offering.

17. My sacrifice [the sacrifice acceptable] to God is a broken spirit; a broken and a contrite heart [broken down with sorrow for sin and humbly and thoroughly penitent], such, O God, you will not despise.

18. Do good in your good pleasure to Zion; rebuild the walls of Jerusalem.

19. Then will you delight in the sacrifices of righteousness, justice, and right, with burnt offering and whole burnt offering; then bullocks will be offered upon your altar.

The Legacy

Janice Pettaway

Two days after her final journal entry, on the way to a Christian youth rally, Dana lost her mortal life in a car accident. However, through the writings of this journal and the testimonies of the people she influenced, it was clear that Dana loved God more than life itself. She gave her life to Him through self-less service and undaunted trust. In her December 24 entry she states, "You are the most important thing in life – I would give it all up for you, my savior." She purposed to become more and more Christ-like, to live out God's will, not her own, and to allow Him to use her to introduce as many as she could to the saving knowledge of Jesus Christ.

The Day God Called Her Home

The last time I laid eyes on my daughter was January 18, 2001, the day of the accident. She was so beautiful that morning – radiant! She was excited about the day, as her Student Venture Christian club was meeting after school, to be followed by a car trip with three church friends to attend a youth rally in Columbus, Texas, where Rod Parsley, a well-known evangelist was going to speak. She was eager to arrive at school early that morning so she and the other leaders of the club could pray for the success of the after-school meeting. While I drove her to school, the ride was unusually quiet as the sweet presence of the Holy Spirit accompanied us. I pulled up to the school and felt the desire to spend more time with her. She gathered up her books, we exchanged "I love you's," and as she got out of the car and walked towards the door, I whispered, "Use her Lord."

Late that evening, our pastors came to our home to inform us of the accident, which occurred on the way to Columbus. The car had hydroplaned on wet pavement, spun, hit a guardrail, and ignited into flames. Dana and the young lady who was driving both perished on the scene. The two other friends managed to escape the car, though they sustained life-threatening burns. We thank God they are both doing well today and living for Him. One of the survivors mentioned that the girls were singing praise songs seconds before impact. It brought to mind Dana's July 17 journal entry: "Lord, I pray that I would be on fire for you until the day that I die. I pray that I would trust, love and hunger for you until I stop breathing." And that she did!

We count it a blessing from the Lord that He used our pastors, compassionate, supportive friends, to deliver the gut-wrenching news. As we were trying to process this horrible news, our pastors were filling our home with prayer and comforting support while making the necessary arrangements. Through them, God had already begun His providential care, which would sustain and carry us through.

We were told that Dana was the main speaker at the Student Venture meeting that day, and shared her faith with a friend who became a Christian! The Lord quickly reminded me of the prayer I whispered as she got out of the car that morning, "Use her Lord."His ways certainly aren't our ways, but use her He did! Dana's earthly mission was fulfilled and complete, and yet her legacy continues to grow.

A Message of Hope and Life

Receiving the news that fateful evening was almost unbearable. In an instant, we found ourselves in the "club" no parent wants to join. The part of us that interacted with Dana on a daily basis would now be empty and inactive. Our lives were changed forever. Though it was difficult to pray, we knew we needed God more than ever to get through the tough times ahead. In our desperation, and with the prayer support of others, we managed to muster up enough faith to cry out. Immediately, our faithful God moved in and took us to a new height of sensitivity to His spirit. He met us daily with His presence. He answered our questions and gave us peace about the things we did not understand. He wrote the obituary and told us what to say in conversations we were *going* to have. He gave us specific instructions regarding the activity and events surrounding her home-going services and subsequent burial. No stone was left unturned. We were experiencing a side of God we had never known!

By far the most comforting Word He gave me was the biblical truth that Dana was with Him. He told us to trust Him – that He had great purpose: A message of Hope and Life – an abundant life of both tangible and intangible benefits through loving and serving Him, and to spread faith that rests on the promise of eternal life to all who believe. That was the message, and it was our charge to see to it that it was conveyed through this seemingly hopeless occurrence.

Many commented on how amazing it was that Curtis and I were ministering to others during that time (as we still do), but it was God's strength and power working through us as part of the purpose. Though our flesh ached to hold Dana again, God's presence was so strong that both Curtis and I admitted we were honored that He chose and trusted us for such a walk. Honored? Paul says it best in *II Corinthians 12:9 (NIV), "But he said to me, 'My grace is sufficient for you, for my power is made perfect in weakness.' Therefore I will boast all the more gladly about my weaknesses, so that Christ's power may rest on me."*

Would God show himself as strongly to you as he did to us? Romans 2:11 tells us that God is no respecter of persons, meaning He shows no partiality. And II Chronicles 16:9 (NIV) states, *"The eyes of the Lord search the whole earth in order to strengthen those whose hearts are fully committed to him..."*

He created you and will strengthen you for his specific purpose. We can all (both young and old) know the Lord in this intensely personal way if we earnestly seek him and ask him to come into our lives with a humble heart.

The Fruit

More than 1,000 people attended her memorial services, which celebrated Dana's life and praised an awesome God who had a place in heaven prepared for his saint. During the youth memorial service, many young people approached the altar with hands raised, surrendering their lives to Jesus. After the main funeral service, many adults admitted reevaluating their relationship with God. The week after Dana's death, attendance at Student Venture increased from 25 to 70 students, and many made decisions for Christ.

One month later, a friend in my Bible study group felt led to donate $5,000 to help buy "Student Survival Kits" in Dana's memory. Each boxed gift included items that helped introduce students to Christ. Students in the Student Venture club, along with Student Venture staff, distributed 350 kits! A senior basketball player whom Dana impacted, eager to reach out to his team, gathered 17 other basketball players for a meeting, distributed kits, and shared the Gospel. Many made decisions for Christ and even attended follow-up Bible studies. That same friend is still living for God and involved with Student Venture at the staff level at another high school.

Another Student Venture staff member met with 35 baseball players, distributed Survival Kits, and shared the Gospel. Again, more decisions for Christ were made and a senior student led a follow-up Bible study for the team.

Student Venture at Dana's high school continued to grow, averaging 40 to 50 students per meeting. Some of them started their own Bible studies, resulting in youth from many different backgrounds coming to Christ. (See her April 14th journal entry that refers to her attending this new high school.) Today, 10 years later, the club still thrives, changing the lives of many teenagers. It is amazing what God can do through one person!

A Challenge to Us All

Dana made every day count in her quest for more of God and her service to others for Him. Even despite many hurts and hardships, she was not defeated. She responded to those challenges with quiet trust in God and His promises. I truly believe that she was aware of the brevity of her life, as, on a couple of occasions as I talked about possibilities for the future, she stated, "I'm not going to be here for that." At age 16, Dana ran her race as if there were no tomorrow. With a strong sense of urgency, she accomplished more for God in her lifetime than many adults do!

The Plan is simple — God sent His Son to die for our sins, and we must confess our sins, receive His forgiveness, and choose to live a life pleasing to Him. We all have a responsibility to run our race with endurance and respond to God's love for us with obedience, faith, and humility. Instruction for this is found in His Word — the Holy Bible. Dana used the Bible as her roadmap for this life, and the way to life eternal.

We are thankful to God that Dana chose the way of salvation and that she is safe in His arms. But we are also thankful for the countless people, both young and old, who were and still are being moved to the point of change in their own lives. Her example challenges us all to ask the following questions:

1. *Am I living life as if each day could be my last?*
2. *Am I living out God's priorities so I leave a legacy for Christ that will grow after I'm gone?*
3. *Am I willing to die to myself daily so others and I will experience Christ's resurrection power?*

It is our prayer and hope that your spirit is quickened to seek God with all your heart and that you surrender your will so that His perfect will can be accomplished in your life.

1 Timothy 4:12 (NIV)

"Don't let anyone look down on you because you are young, but set an example for the believers in speech, in life, in love, in faith and in purity."

About This Ministry

Dana Michelle Pettaway Ministries (DMP Ministries.org) was established in January 2004 by Dana's parents, Curtis and Janice Pettaway. It captures the essence of the heart Dana had for God and others, and continues her ministry of mentorship.

Mission Statement: To change the world for Christ, one person at a time by promoting, mentoring and encouraging people to live for God and to utilize their God-given talents in loving service to others.

DMP Ministries is a nonprofit, 501(c)3, head-quartered in Houston, Texas. Donations are tax deductible and may be earmarked. Check website often for upcoming events and programs.

Dana Michelle Pettaway Ministries
6430 Cypress Creek Parkway, #117
Houston, TX 77069

DMPMinistries.org
DMPMinistries@att.net

Dana's Family

Dana's parents, Curtis and Janice Pettaway, and brother, Curtis, Jr., reside in Houston, Texas. Curtis is an academic urologic oncologist at the University of Texas M.D. Anderson Cancer Center. Janice is actively involved in the Dana Michelle Pettaway Ministries, and both serve as leaders in church ministry. "CJ" is pursuing his education and career in the music industry.